# MUCH ADO ABOUT NOTHING

## AN AQA ESSAY WRITING GUIDE

### BY MIRANDA MATTHEWS
### SERIES EDITOR: R. P. DAVIS

First published in 2020 by Accolade Tuition Ltd
71-75 Shelton Street
Covent Garden
London WC2H 9JQ
www.accoladetuition.com
info@accoladetuition.com

ISBN 978-1-913988-03-6

FIRST EDITION
1 3 5 7 9 10 8 6 4 2

# CONTENTS

# EDITOR'S FOREWORD

In your GCSE English Literature exam, you will be presented with an extract from Shakespeare's *Much Ado About Nothing* and a question that asks you to offer both a close analysis of the extract plus a commentary of the play as a whole. Of course, there are many methods one *might* use to tackle this style of question. However, there is one particular technique which, due to its sophistication, most readily allows students to unlock the highest marks: namely, **the thematic method**.

To be clear, this study guide is *not* intended to walk you through the play scene-by-scene: there are many great guides out there that do just that. No, this guide, by sifting through a series of mock exam questions, will demonstrate *how* to organise a response thematically and thus write a stellar essay: a skill we believe no other study guide adequately covers!

I have encountered students who have structured their essays all sorts of ways: some by writing about the extract line by line, others by identifying various language techniques and giving each its own paragraph. The method I'm advocating, on the other hand, involves picking out three to four themes that will allow you to holistically answer the question: these three to four themes will become the three to four content paragraphs of your essay, cushioned between a brief introduction and conclusion. Ideally, these themes will follow from one to the next to create a flowing argument. Within each of these thematic paragraphs, you can then ensure you are jumping through the mark scheme's hoops.

So to break things down further, each thematic paragraph will include various point-scoring components. In each paragraph, you will quote from the extract, offer analyses of these quotes, then discuss how the specific language techniques you have identified illustrate the theme you're discussing. In each paragraph, you will also discuss how other parts of the play further illustrate the theme (or even complicate it). And in each, you will comment on the era in which the play was written and how that helps to understand the chosen theme.

Don't worry if this all feels daunting. Throughout this guide, the very talented Miranda (the author!) will be illustrating in great detail – by means of examples – how to build an essay of this kind.

The beauty of the thematic approach is that, once you have your themes, you suddenly have a direction and a trajectory, and this makes essay writing a whole lot

The Shakespearian equivalent of a selfie.

easier. However, it must also be noted that extracting themes in the first place is something students often find tricky. I have come across many candidates who understand the extract and the play inside out; but when they are presented with a question under exam conditions, and the pressure kicks in, they find it tough to break their response down into themes. The fact of the matter is: the process is a *creative* one and the best themes require a bit of imagination.

In this guide, Miranda shall take seven different exam-style questions, coupled with extracts from the play, and put together a plan for each – a plan that illustrates in detail how we will be satisfying the mark scheme's criteria. Please do keep in mind that, when operating under timed conditions, your plans will necessarily be less detailed than those that appear in this volume.

Now, you might be asking whether three or four themes is best. The truth is, you should do whatever you feel most comfortable with: the examiner is looking for an original, creative answer, and not sitting there counting the themes. So if you think you are quick enough to cover four, then great. However, if you would rather do three to make sure you do each theme justice, that's also fine. I sometimes suggest that my student pick four themes, but make the fourth one smaller – sort of like an afterthought, or an observation that turns things on their head. That way, if they feel they won't have time to explore this fourth theme in its own right, they can always give it a quick mention in the conclusion instead.

The Globe Theatre, London. It was built on the site of the original, which was burnt down in 1613.

Before I hand you over to Miranda, I believe it to be worthwhile to run through the four Assessment Objectives the exam board want you to cover in your response – if only to demonstrate how effective the thematic response can be. I would argue that the first Assessment Objective (AO1) – the one that wants candidates to 'read, understand and respond to texts' and which is worth 12 of the total 34 marks up for grabs – will be wholly satisfied by selecting strong themes, then fleshing them out with quotes. Indeed, when it comes to identifying the top-scoring candidates for AO1, the mark scheme explicitly tells examiners to look for a 'critical, exploratory, conceptualised response' that makes 'judicious use of precise references' – the word 'concept' is a synonym of theme, and 'judicious references' simply refers to quotes that appropriately support the theme you've chosen.

The second Assessment Objective (AO2) – which is also

responsible for 12 marks – asks students to 'analyse the language, form and structure used by a writer to create meanings and effects, using relevant subject terminology where appropriate.' As noted, you will already be quoting from the play as you back up your themes, and it is a natural progression to then analyse the language techniques used. In fact, this is far more effective than simply observing language techniques (personification here, alliteration there), because by discussing how the language techniques relate to and shape the theme, you will also be demonstrating how the writer 'create[s] meanings and effects.'

Now, in my experience, language analysis is the most important element of AO2 – perhaps 8 of the 12 marks will go towards language analysis. You will also notice, however, that AO2 asks students to comment on 'form and structure.' Again, the thematic approach has your back – because though simply jamming in a point on form or structure will feel jarring, when you bring these points up while discussing a theme, as a means to further a thematic argument, you will again organically be discussing the way it 'create[s] meanings and effects.'

AO3 requires you to 'show understanding of the relationships between texts and the contexts in which they were written' and is responsible for a more modest 6 marks in total. These are easy enough to weave into a thematic argument; indeed, the theme gives the student a chance to bring up context in a relevant and fitting way. After all, you don't want it to look like you've just shoehorned a contextual factoid into the mix.

Finally, you have AO4 – known also as "spelling and grammar." There are four marks up for grabs here. Truth be told, this guide is not geared towards AO4. My advice? Make sure you are reading plenty of books and articles, because the more you read, the better your spelling and grammar will be. Also, before the exam, perhaps make a list of words you struggle to spell but often find yourself using in essays, and commit them to memory.

| The Globe Theatre's interior.

My (and Miranda's!) hope is that this book, by demonstrating how to tease out themes from an extract, will help you feel more confident in doing so yourself. I believe it is also worth mentioning that the themes I have picked out are by no means definitive. Asked the very same question, someone else may pick out different themes, and write an answer that is just as good (if not better!). Obviously the exam is not likely to be fun – my memory of them is pretty much the exact opposite. But still, this is one of the very few chances that you will get at GCSE level to actually be creative. And to my mind at least, that was always more enjoyable – if *enjoyable* is the right word

– than simply demonstrating that I had memorised loads of facts.

**R. P. Davis, Series Editor**

READ THE FOLLOWING EXTRACT FROM
ACT 1 SCENE 1 OF MUCH ADO ABOUT
NOTHING AND THEN ANSWER THE
QUESTION THAT FOLLOWS.

**AT THIS POINT in the play, Claudio has just encountered Hero for the first time.**

**CLAUDIO**
Benedick, didst thou note the daughter of Signior
    Leonato?
**BENEDICK**
I noted her not; but I looked on her.
**CLAUDIO**
Is she not a modest young lady?
**BENEDICK**
Do you question me, as an honest man should do, for
    my simple true judgment; or would you have me
    speak after my custom, as being a professed tyrant
    to their sex?
**CLAUDIO**
No; I pray thee speak in sober judgment.
**BENEDICK**
Why, i' faith, methinks she's too low for a high praise,

too brown for a fair praise and too little for a great praise: only this commendation I can afford her, that were she other than she is, she were unhandsome; and being no other but as she is, I do not like her.

**CLAUDIO**

Thou thinkest I am in sport: I pray thee tell me truly how thou likest her.

**BENEDICK**

Would you buy her, that you inquire after her?

**CLAUDIO**

Can the world buy such a jewel?

**BENEDICK**

Yea, and a case to put it into.

---

**Starting with this conversation, discuss how Shakespeare presents male attitudes to romantic love in the play.**

**Write about:**

**• how Shakespeare presents male attitudes to romantic love in this extract**

**• how Shakespeare presents male attitudes to romantic love in the play as a whole**

---

### Introduction

It's often a good idea to kick your essay off with some historical context, since it will ensure you'll be scoring some AO3 marks off the bat. I'd then suggest quickly touching on the themes you're planning to cover in the essay, as I've done below.

---

"At the end of the sixteenth century there was a dichotomy between the idea of romantic love, which was still influenced by the medieval chivalric code of knights and their ladies, and the reality of contemporary courtship and marriage.[1] In this patriarchal society the male head of the family made matches for financial or dynastic, rather than romantic, reasons.[2] These attitudes, along with Benedick's initial portrayal as a romantic sceptic, are variously presented in the play."

---

**Theme/Paragraph One: Shakespeare uses Claudio to present an overly-naive attitude towards romance: an attitude which places a love interest on an unrealistic pedestal, and which is in keeping with the courtly tradition..**

- We know from Leonato's early words: 'Don Pedro hath bestowed much honour on a young Florentine called Claudio' that when Don Pedro and his entourage arrive in Messina, it is the first time Claudio has encountered Hero. Yet he falls in love with her immediately. This "love at first sight" is in the tradition of courtly love and establishes Claudio as naive and credulous. Indeed, his misty-eyed question, 'Can the world buy such a jewel?', indicates that he has formed an idealised and unrealistic perception of

Hero: he sees her as almost otherworldly. Ironically, he begs Benedick to 'speak in sober judgment,' yet his own judgment appears to be highly questionable. [*AO1 for advancing the argument with a judiciously selected quote; AO2 for the close analysis of the language; AO3 for placing the text in historical context*].

- As a result of elevating Hero to a nearly goddess-like status, and thus implicitly casting his courtship as a transcendental undertaking, Claudio's approach to romance becomes fraught with nerves and insecurity: Claudio several times interjects nervously into Benedick's facetious speeches, hoping for his friend's approval and guidance ('Is she not a modest young lady?'; tell me truly how much thou likest her').[3] [*AO1 for advancing the argument with a judiciously selected quote*].

- *Elsewhere in the play*: Curiously, although Benedick appears to take the more openly misogynistic stance in this extract, it in fact transpires that Claudio's approach to romance, which posits absurd standards for a love interest to live up to, leads to greater misogyny. [4] When Claudio later believes the worst of Hero, he scathingly proclaims that 'Her blush is guiltiness, not modesty.' Shakespeare shows that the greater the illusion, the greater the disillusion in this form of romantic love. [*AO1 for advancing the argument with a judiciously selected quote*].

**Theme/Paragraph Two: Through Benedick, Shakespeare presents a far more jocular – and perhaps even cynical – attitude towards romantic love: Benedick appears to see it as 'a sport.'**

- Whereas Claudio in this extract approaches romantic love with deathly seriousness, Benedick takes the attitude that romance is an excuse for jocularity.[5] He is happy to indulge in wordplay rather than reassuring his friend. When Benedick says 'I noted her not, but I looked on her,' Shakespeare could be reminding us of the punning title of the play; 'Nothing' was pronounced similarly to 'Noting' and its near-homophone had many meanings: gossiping, eavesdropping, rumour-mongering, and the euphemisms for male and female sexual parts: thing and no-thing.[6] Benedick uses the wordplay of contrary opposites: low, high, brown, fair, little, great in a rhythmic speech which ends with the bald, staccato phrase 'I do not like her', creating a comic effect. [*AO1 for advancing the argument with a judiciously selected quote; AO2 for the close analysis of the language*].
- *Elsewhere in the play*: Benedick's jocular attitude to romantic love seems to be echoed in the stance of Don Pedro, who, despite encouraging romantic matches, is happy to promote love by using trickery. When he devises the plot to bring Benedick and Beatrice together and says alliteratively 'I...will so practice upon Benedick that in despite of his quick wit and his queasy stomach, he shall fall in love with Beatrice,' there is irony in the idea of the joker becoming the victim of the joke. [*AO1 for advancing the argument with a judiciously selected quote*].
- Yet while it might be tempting to construe Benedick's attitude as cynical, there is considerable irony and self-awareness when he refers to himself as 'a

professed tyrant to their [the female] sex.' Indeed, his realism and his understanding of female fallibility ultimately inoculates him against the sort of misogyny that Don John's chicanery reveals in Claudio.[7] A sister or cousin's sexual disgrace could severely harm the reputations of every female in the family, at least until the nineteenth century, as can be seen in Jane Austen's *Pride and Prejudice* when Lydia Bennett elopes unmarried and her sisters assume that is the end of their own marital prospects. Yet Benedick, far from deserting Beatrice when Hero is slandered, seeks her out and supports her. [*AO1 for advancing the argument with a judiciously selected quote; AO3 for placing the text in historical context*].

**Theme/Paragraph Three: Shakespeare presents male attitudes towards romantic love as belonging to the public sphere: the men of Messina are expected to have views on romantic love and to feel comfortable airing them in public.**

- At the outset of this extract, Claudio places pressure on Benedick to air his views on Hero – and, tacitly, romantic engagements in general. However, Benedick's response, which sees him ask whether Claudio wants him to express his 'simple true judgement' or 'speak after [his] custom,' hints at a striking reality: that Benedick, conscious that he would be solicited for his views on romantic love, has cultivated a persona that he deploys as a mouthpiece for his views – a persona that is potentially at odds with his private thoughts. Benedick's equivocations throughout this passage might be less to do with scepticism towards romance, and more a mark of frustration that he is expected to have a stance on the subject at all.[8] [*AO1 for advancing the argument with a judiciously selected quote; AO2 for the close analysis of the language*].

- That this expectation on men to express their views on romantic engagement is revealed in the play's opening sequence gives it structural emphasis: it readies the audience to expect it as a persistent motif throughout the play. [*AO2 for discussing how structure shapes meaning*].

- *Elsewhere in the play*: Indeed, as the play unfolds, the patriarchal realm of Messina as a whole is one in which men are expected to air their views on romance. Don John, when conversing with loyalists, makes no bones about his anti-romantic worldview. Moreover, in Act 1, Scene 2, Leonato airs his views that romance must be subjugated to political expedience when he brusquely tells Hero: 'If the Prince do solicit you in that kind, you know your answer.' Interestingly, in that same sequence, Beatrice is at liberty to also air her views on romance, yet Hero remains conspicuously mum. Women may be permitted to share their views; but, in this patriarchal domain, their voices are considered unintegral and secondary: their 'answer' is ultimately the one foisted on them by patriarchal forces. [*AO1 for advancing the argument with a judiciously selected quote*].

## Conclusion

"The attitudes of Shakespeare's two male lovers are portrayed as ephemeral, because both of them undergo profound changes on their journey towards married happiness.[9] Benedick's and Beatrice's verbal sparring, reminiscent of the stormy relationship of Katherine and Petruchio in *The Taming Of The Shrew*, is abandoned when each is tricked into believing the other loves them, and Benedick has his epiphany. Once he says 'Love me! Why, it must be requited...I will be horribly in love with her,' his sceptical attitude is permanently reversed. Claudio, seemingly the more romantic of the two, proves disloyal when Hero is slandered, and treats her cruelly. When he finally marries Hero, it is hard to believe the marriage will be happy unless he has changed again, lost his imagined ideal, and accepted her as a woman, not a goddess."

A photo of Laure Hope Crews and John Drew portraying Beatrice and Benedick in a 1913 production of *Much Ado About Nothing* at New York's Empire Theatre.

READ THE FOLLOWING EXTRACT FROM
ACT 1 SCENE 3 OF MUCH ADO ABOUT
NOTHING AND THEN ANSWER THE
QUESTION THAT FOLLOWS.

**AT THIS POINT in the play, Don John, after recently
being introduced to Leonato's court, is speaking
candidly to his followers.**

### DON JOHN

I cannot hide what I am: I must be sad when I have
cause and smile at no man's jests, eat when I have
stomach and wait for no man's leisure, sleep when I
am drowsy and tend on no man's business, laugh
when I am merry and claw no man in his humour.

### CONRADE

Yea, but you must not make the full show of this till you
may do it without controlment. You have of late
stood out against your brother, and he hath ta'en
you newly into his grace; where it is impossible you
should take true root but by the fair weather that
you make yourself: it is needful that you frame the
season for your own harvest.

### DON JOHN

I had rather be a canker in a hedge than a rose in his
    grace, and it better fits my blood to be disdained of
    all than to fashion a carriage to rob love from any: in
    this, though I cannot be said to be a flattering honest
    man, it must not be denied but I am a plain-dealing
    villain. I am trusted with a muzzle and enfranchised
    with a clog; therefore I have decreed not to sing in
    my cage. If I had my mouth, I would bite; if I had
    my liberty, I would do my liking: in the meantime
    let me be that I am and seek not to alter me.

---

**Starting with this extract, explore how
Shakespeare presents Don John as a villain
in *Much Ado About Nothing*.**

**Write about:**

• **how Shakespeare presents Don John as a
villain in this extract**

• **how Shakespeare presents Don John as a
villain in the play as a whole**

---

## Introduction

Although I generally like to use my introduction to score early
AO3 (context) marks, you can also use the introduction to nab
other marks that students all too frequently let fall through the
cracks. On this occasion, I have started with a point on structure, which will score us those AO2 marks that language analysis
alone will not secure.

---

"This dialogue, coming at the end of Act One in the play's structure, introduces the audience to Don John's character and intentions, setting up the non-romantic plotline of the drama. This reveal heightens the dramatic tension for the following Act; as Don Pedro merrily plans the match of Hero and Claudio, the audience knows that there is 'a canker in the hedge.' Shakespeare arguably presents Don John here as a villain who believes he has a right, and more than one excuse, to be villainous, and is quite content to be as he is: '...seek not to alter me.'"

---

**Theme/Paragraph One: Don John is presented as villainous insofar as he is choosing to repay Don Pedro's forgiveness and trust with disdain and cruelty.**

- It might seem that only a most charitable and forbearing half-brother would immediately forgive a sibling who had raised a rebellion against him and killed some of his men – however expendable – in the process. Conrade points out that Don Pedro 'hath ta'en you newly into his grace'; but far from appreciating his position, Don John feels resentment and bitterness at having to be in his half-brother's debt. It can be observed that the only reason Don John appears to have for remaining at Don Pedro's side is to be able to hurt him; since his 'honest' method of warfare failed, he feels compelled to do him another kind of damage, by destroying his protégé's happiness. [*AO1 for advancing the argument with a judiciously selected quote*].

- Elsewhere in the play: Don John's hatred of Claudio – the 'very forward March-chick' as he calls him, implying that Claudio has ambitions beyond his abilities – appears to be partly transferred hatred of his half-brother, but could also be interpreted as presenting another classic trait of the villain: jealousy. Despite seemingly loathing his brother, Don John could be wishing to be the favourite himself, with attendant privileges, in the rightful place of a brother. [*AO1 for advancing the argument with a judiciously selected quote; AO2 for the close analysis of the language*].

**Theme/Paragraph Two: Arguably Don John's chief reason for misery is at having to hide his true saturnine personality.[1] He explicitly presents himself as a villain, and if his self-assessment is to be believed, his villainy is inescapable. Yet he seems to take no great pleasure in his machinations.[2]**

- Shakespeare presents Don John in this passage as a villain who is furious at having to maintain '..a patient sufferance' as his follower suggests. His view of himself is made clear in the oxymoronic wordplay of admitting he is not 'a flattering honest man' but rather 'a plain-dealing villain' and he accepts his villainy as his natural character when he says 'I cannot hide what I am'.[3] His dislike of being unable to show his true villainous colours might be emphasised so that the audience may imagine how badly he wishes revenge on Don Pedro if he is prepared to act the unnatural part of a reformed man. [*AO1 for advancing the argument with a judiciously selected quote; AO2 for the close analysis of the language*].

- Unusually among Shakespeare's villains, however, Don John does not appear to enjoy deception and intrigue for its own sake as well as for its ultimate achievement. He has no soliloquies which revel in concealment, as when Richard The Third tells the audience he delights in being 'Subtle, false and treacherous', or when Iago in *Othello* boasts that 'Knavery's plain face is never seen till used'. Don John pays others to do his dirty work – promising Borachio a thousand ducats for his deception – where enthusiastic villains might prefer to be more directly involved in the action themselves. [*AO3 for placing the text in literary context*].

**Theme/Paragraph Three: Shakespeare uses the trope of the illegitimate malcontent to convey Don John's villainy; in his canon illegitimacy is often deployed as shorthand for villainy. By emphasising the virtues of the legitimate sibling, the wickedness of the illegitimate one is underlined. However, it may be that Don John's behaviour seems more excusable, since his lashing out could be deemed a natural reaction to his unfair treatment since birth.**

- Illegitimate progeny caused trouble in Greek mythology – Zeus had numerous bastards by various mortal and immortal women – and there have been many historical instances of illegitimate sons who have grown up to rebel against their legitimate relatives, from Thomas of Galloway in the twelfth century to the Duke of Monmouth, the bastard son of Charles II. Illegitimacy came to symbolise villainy in Shakespeare's dramas, and both Edmund in *King Lear* and Don John exemplify this metaphor. [*AO3 for placing the text in literary and historical context*].

- Notably, Don John himself brings to mind his bloodline when he asserts that it 'fits [his] blood to be disdained of all.' Not only, then, does he self-identify as a villain, but he also suggests that villainy 'fits' the nature of his illegitimate blood; that his villainy is inescapably predestined by the circumstances of birth. This direct link between bastardry and villainy is a sentiment echoed later by Benedick, who talks of 'John the bastard, / Whose spirits toil in frame of villanies.' The close proximity of the moniker 'John the bastard' and his 'villanies,' each situated as they are at the end of a line of verse, not-so-subtly invites the audience to draw a link between them.[4] [*AO1 for advancing the argument with a judiciously selected quote; AO2 for the close analysis of the language*].

- However, while Don John's illegitimacy might be said to further his presentation as a villain, it may also engender some sympathy for Don John's position, as a man who has felt undervalued since birth. Indeed, comparison with his legitimate half-sibling, who finds it easy to be cheerful and benevolent because of his innate privileged position, appears clearly unfair, and when Hero says 'He is of a very melancholy disposition' the audience can understand why that might be so. [*AO1 for advancing the argument with a judiciously selected quote*].

## Conclusion

---

"Shakespeare could be said to present Don John as a "complete" villain because he appears to be villainous both by nature and nurture: a villain due to his unhappy birth circumstances, his naturally unsociable and malign personality, and his learnt bitterness and resentment against not only his more fortunate half-brother, but against all those associated with him. He regards himself as an "honest" villain but that self-assessment is hard to accept when one considers that he heartlessly uses deception to effect the downfall and pro facto death of an innocent young woman, simply as collateral damage in his scheme to hurt Don Pedro. There are echoes here of the machinations of the arch-villain Iago, the instigator of Desdemona's death in *Othello*."

---

A statue of Shakespeare in Stratford-upon-Avon, the town in which he was born.

READ THE FOLLOWING EXTRACT FROM
ACT 2 SCENE 1 OF MUCH ADO ABOUT
NOTHING AND THEN ANSWER THE
QUESTION THAT FOLLOWS.

**AT THIS POINT in the play, Hero and Claudio's marriage has been arranged and Don Pedro is planning his next venture.**

**DON PEDRO**

I will in the interim undertake one of Hercules' labours;
 which is, to bring Signior Benedick and the Lady
 Beatrice into a mountain of affection the one with
 the other. I would fain have it a match, and I doubt
 not but to fashion it, if you three will but minister
 such assistance as I shall give you direction.

**LEONATO**

My lord, I am for you, though it cost me ten nights'
 watchings.

**CLAUDIO**

And I, my lord.

**DON PEDRO**

And you too, gentle Hero?

**HERO**

I will do any modest office, my lord, to help my cousin
to a good husband.

**DON PEDRO**

And Benedick is not the unhopefullest husband that I
know. Thus far can I praise him; he is of a noble
strain, of approved valour and confirmed honesty. I
will teach you how to humour your cousin, that she
shall fall in love with Benedick; and I, with your
two helps, will so practise on Benedick that, in
despite of his quick wit and his queasy stomach, he
shall fall in love with Beatrice. If we can do this,
Cupid is no longer an archer: his glory shall be
ours, for we are the only love-gods. Go in with me,
and I will tell you my drift.

*Exeunt*

---

**Starting with this extract, explore how far
Shakespeare presents Don Pedro as a
matchmaker in the play.**

**Write about:**

**• how far Shakespeare presents Don Pedro
as a matchmaker in this extract**

**• how far Shakespeare presents Don Pedro
as as a matchmaker in the play as a whole**

---

## Introduction

Once again, you'll notice that I start the essay with historical
context, thereby immediately picking up marks. I then use the

commentary on how marriage was construed in Shakespeare's time as a springboard to start discussing the themes I intend to cover, and, in so doing, set myself up to start scoring AO1 points.

---

Although mutual consent by the couple concerned was becoming more common, in the patriarchal society of the sixteenth and seventeenth centuries, marriages of the wealthy were usually arranged by the male head of the family. In *Much Ado about Nothing*, Don Pedro is able to influence Hero's marriage because he is a Prince of Spain and thus outranks Leonato, the local governor. As Don Pedro is also presented as enjoying matchmaking as an entertainment in itself, it makes sense that most of the characters in the play follow his lead whenever he "would fain have it a match".

---

**Theme/Paragraph One: Don Pedro is presented as a matchmaker insofar as he takes pains to cast himself as the matchmaker-in-chief among his entourage, and this effort appears to become a self-fulfilling prophecy: those around him wind up following his lead.**

- In this extract Don Pedro seems confident, after his recent part in successfully bringing about the betrothal between Claudio and Hero, that he can do the same with the seemingly ill-matched pair of Beatrice and Benedick: 'I doubt not but to fashion it...' In two classical allusions he compares himself first to

Hercules, with his superhuman strength, and then to Cupid, the god of love – he is compellingly portraying himself as having a near-divine touch for matchmaking.[1] His three confederate "Love Gods" in this plan are eager to take part in it, before they even know what it will entail – even Hero, who might be expected to be suspicious of any trick played on her cousin, agrees to join in. This attests to Don Pedro's enthusiasm and powers of persuasion as he seeks to take the mantle of arch matchmaker. [*AO1 for advancing the argument with a judiciously selected quote; AO2 for the close analysis of the language; AO3 for placing the text in literary context*].

- That this passage constitutes the end of the scene structurally reinforces the sense of Don Pedro actively taking the lead as chief matchmaker, and seducing others to dance to his tune: it ensures he has the final word, while his authoritative 'Go with me' is given symbolic resonance as all the characters then 'exeunt.' [*AO1 for advancing the argument with a judiciously selected quote; AO2 for discussing how structure shapes meaning*].

- *Elsewhere in the play*: It appears that Don Pedro is self-consciously casting himself as matchmaker from the beginning of the play when Benedick declares he will never marry. 'I shall see thee, ere I die, look pale with love' claims the Prince, and eventually he is proved right through his own machinations. [*AO1 for advancing the argument with a judiciously selected quote*].

**Theme/Paragraph Two: Don Pedro could arguably be understood primarily as a benign**

**trickster; and while matchmaking appears to be his aim, it seems secondary to the trickery itself, which he enjoys enormously as long as it leads to a happy ending.**

- It can be argued that some of Don Pedro's matchmaking schemes are unnecessarily risky if not underhand, and appear more designed to amuse himself than to promote stable marriages. In this extract his ideas are becoming somewhat grandiose, as he imagines bringing Benedick and Beatrice 'into a mountain of affection th' one with th' other', the elisions showing his haste and excitement with his growing plan.[2] That trickery is front and centre of his mind is also betrayed when he talks of inducing Benedick to fall for Beatrice 'in despite of his quick wits:' Don Pedro sees it as an opportunity to pit the 'quick wits' of his trickery against Benedick's intelligence. [*AO1 for advancing the argument with a judiciously selected quote; AO2 for the close analysis of the language*].

- There is a parallel here with the mischief-making of Oberon and Puck in *A Midsummer Night's Dream*, where the use of magic, as opposed to deception and trickery, is used to bring about some unlikely and chaotic romantic relationships. Don Pedro decides, unasked, to disguise himself as Claudio in order to woo Hero; this nearly causes disaster when Don John tells Claudio that Don Pedro is interested in Hero for himself. Bringing Benedick and Beatrice together by means of lying and deception could also have ended badly – but Don Pedro seems to think the end justifies any means necessary, as long as he is entertained. [*AO3 for placing the text in literary context*].

- *Elsewhere in the play*: Taking responsibility for the results of his matchmaking plans does not seem to be part of Don Pedro's character – again, suggesting that matchmaking is secondary to the trickery. When he believes Hero to be unfaithful, he addresses Claudio: 'And, as I wooed for thee to obtain her, I will join with thee to disgrace her.' On his arrival at the second wedding, despite believing Hero to be dead, he is back to his old, jovial self and teases Benedick for looking sad while apparently unaffected by the tragedy himself. [*AO1 for advancing the argument with a judiciously selected quote*].

**Theme/Paragraph Three: Arguably, by high-lighting Don Pedro's ability to see beyond Benedick and Beatrice's affectations and recognise their potential as a couple, Shakespeare implicitly presents Don Pedro as a skilled matchmaker.**

- Shakespeare tells us that Don Pedro and his entourage have lately come from battle. We do not know his age, but as he sometimes addresses Leonato as 'Old man', and as he is clearly not a youth like Claudio and Benedict, it appears that he is in middle age; as a royal prince and a fighting soldier he must have much life experience and probably an understanding of people's characters and their relationships. He knows Benedick well and praises him: 'He is of a noble strain, of approved valour, and confirm'd honesty' and we may deduce that he sees

Benedick's misogyny as the affectation it later proves, as he calls him 'Not the unhopefullest husband I know.'[3] [AO1 *for advancing the argument with a judiciously selected quote*].

- Equally, Don Pedro has shown he is intrigued by Beatrice's outspoken liveliness when he called her 'A pleasant-spirited lady' and arguably he can see that the barbed repartee between the young people is actually a form of flirting – much as Oberon and Titania in *A Midsummer Night's Dream* bicker on the surface while being deeply attracted to each other. As a result, one might surmise that Don Pedro is experienced enough to see Beatrice and Benedict are actually an excellent match for each other – even though they are initially unable to see this themselves. It is thus through Don Pedro's perceptiveness that Shakespeare tacitly affirms Don Pedro's matchmaking prowess. [AO1 *for advancing the argument with a judiciously selected quote; AO3 for placing the text in literary context*].

## Conclusion

I have one other point I wish to cover; however, because it's just a small one, I've decided to use it to kick off my conclusion.

---

"Marriage in Elizabethan England was seen as a prerequisite to producing a legitimate heir (such as Don Pedro) as opposed to an illegitimate progeny (such as Don John). As a result, Don Pedro's mere existence arguably speaks to the importance of prudent matchmaking, and tacitly gives legitimacy to his self-anointed role as chief matchmaker. Certainly, he is the principal agent of the two matches made in the play; without him one wonders if the timorous Claudio and Hero, or the belligerent Beatrice and Benedick, would ever have arrived at the altar. Indeed, the latter match was arguably envisaged by him when nobody else could see it, thus showing him to be a shrewd judge of relationships, and both matches are effected eventually, so perhaps he could be said to deserve the "Love-god" status he bestows upon himself."

Shakespeare's home in Stratford-upon-Avon

# ESSAY PLAN FOUR

READ THE FOLLOWING EXTRACT FROM
ACT 3 SCENE 1 OF MUCH ADO ABOUT
NOTHING AND THEN ANSWER THE
QUESTION THAT FOLLOWS.

**AT THIS POINT in the play, Hero prepares to deceive
Beatrice into believing that Benedick loves her.**

### HERO

Good Margaret, run thee to the parlor;
There shalt thou find my cousin Beatrice
Proposing with the prince and Claudio:
Whisper her ear and tell her, I and Ursula
Walk in the orchard and our whole discourse
Is all of her; say that thou overheard'st us;
And bid her steal into the pleached bower,
Where honeysuckles, ripen'd by the sun,
Forbid the sun to enter, like favourites,
Made proud by princes, that advance their pride
Against that power that bred it: there will she hide her,
To listen our purpose. This is thy office;
Bear thee well in it and leave us alone.

### MARGARET

I'll make her come, I warrant you, presently.

*Exit*

**HERO**
Now, Ursula, when Beatrice doth come,
As we do trace this alley up and down,
Our talk must only be of Benedick.
When I do name him, let it be thy part
To praise him more than ever man did merit:
My talk to thee must be how Benedick
Is sick in love with Beatrice. Of this matter
Is little Cupid's crafty arrow made,
That only wounds by hearsay.
*Enter BEATRICE, behind*
Now begin

---

**Starting with this passage, explore how Shakespeare presents deception in the play.**

**Write about:**

**• how Shakespeare presents deception in this extract**

**• how Shakespeare presents deception in the play as a whole**

---

## Introduction

---

"A play in itself can be considered as a grand deception; the sets and scenery deceive the eye, turning a wooden stage into a battlefield, a bedroom or an ornamental garden. Actors deceive when they portray characters, especially so in Shakespeare's time when all women's parts were played by men. The 'women' on stage might then deceive twice by dressing in men's clothes to effect the deceptions within the plot. Most of Shakespeare's dramas contain deceptions that are essential to driving the narrative, and both heroes and villains use deceit to achieve pleasant or unpleasant ends. This excerpt leads in to a deception originally instigated by Don Pedro, who has believed since meeting her that Beatrice 'were an excellent wife for Benedick."

---

**Theme/Paragraph One. In this extract deception is presented as a well-meaning prank, played on Beatrice as a means to a happy ending. The form of language used by Hero shows her status and contrasts with the previous scene at the end of Act Two.**

- This passage at the beginning of Act Three follows the similarly plotted, but wholly masculine, tricking of Benedick by Don Pedro, Leonato and Claudio. This time all the deceivers and the deceived are female, and the language Shakespeare uses is shot through with a delicacy that Elizabethan society associated with femininity. Hero's speeches are written in iambic pentameter, a form Shakespeare uses for aristocratic characters, and the euphonic flow of her words is full of sensuous metaphors and alliteration.[1] Particularly potent is the imagery of the 'honeysuckles, ripened by the sun,' for Shakespeare knew the symbolism of plants and honeysuckle symbolised devoted affection in the form of a lover's embrace. [*AO1 for advancing the argument with a judiciously selected quote; AO2 for the close analysis of the language; AO3 for placing the text in historical context*].

- This deception of Beatrice is presented by Shakespeare as a means to a romantic and joyful ending; it is successful, as Beatrice accepts the lies told as truths, and from then on loves Benedick without question, even when she at last finds out the deception played upon her.

- Elsewhere in the play: The same deception, when practised on Benedick by the three other men at the end of Act Two, has a more macho style. The metaphors are about hunting: 'Stalk on, stalk on; the fowl sits' and fishing: 'Bait the hook well, this fish will bite.' The men tease and talk in innuendoes; when Claudio speaks of a sheet of paper with a love note written on it, Leonato talks of finding '"Benedick" and "Beatrice" between the sheet!'² However, despite some of the grotesqueries that characterise this deception, it does indeed bring about a happy ending: Benedick – like Beatrice – is credulous towards what he hears, and these twin deceptions function in unison to precipitate their happy relationship. [*AO1 for advancing the argument with a judiciously selected quote; AO2 for the close analysis of the language*].

**Theme/Paragraph Two: Although this deception and the deception levelled at Benedick combine to bring about a happy union, there is a distinct lack of consideration by those instigating these decep-**

**tions of the damage that might ensue should their gambit fail.**

- While, as mentioned, Hero talks in iambic pentameter, one might notice that the second line in this extract – 'There shalt thou find my cousin Beatrice' – is in fact a syllable short, and constitutes instead an iambic tetrameter with an unstressed hyperbeat.[3] This, combined with the elisions that punctuate her speech ('overheard'st'; 'ripen'd'), creates a sense of haste: Hero is rushing to get her deception underway. Indeed, in the space of these short lines, Hero goes from putting together a hasty plot to actually putting it into motion ('Now begin'), the structural compactness redoubling the sense of events galloping apace. This hastiness to put together plans obliquely draws attention to the lack of forethought or consideration that goes into Beatrice's feelings – particularly in the event that the gambit should fail. The trick played on the lovers could have a disastrous result if only one of them fell in love as a result of it, and would cause shame and embarrassment if neither did. [*AO1 for advancing the argument with a judiciously selected quote; AO2 for the close analysis of the language and for discussing how structure shapes meaning*].
- Elsewhere in the play: However, not only are those instigating the deception presented as dangerously unthinking, but so too are those on its receiving end. Both Beatrice and Benedick appear to believe easily the lies told by those who deceive them, and this motif recurs through the play. For instance, when Don John's plot against Don Pedro and Claudio unfolds,

nearly all the characters except Beatrice and the Friar are quickly convinced of Hero's infidelity, despite all previous evidence of her goodness and modesty. Shakespeare might be thought to be presenting deception as a means of pointing out the gullibility of people, their ease in believing others love them, and their all-too-human eagerness to believe the worst of others. [*AO1 for advancing the argument with a judiciously selected quote; AO2 for the close analysis of the language; AO3 for placing the text in historical context*].

**Theme/Paragraph Three: Not only are deceptions presented as capable of doing harm as a result of a lack of forethought on the part of the instigators, but they are also presented as a mechanism for *intentionally* exacting punishment. Hero is arguably punishing Beatrice for her anti-romantic views, and Benedick is arguably punished for the same reason.**

- When Hero says to Ursula 'Of this matter is little Cupid's crafty arrow made, which only wounds by hearsay' it might be considered that 'only' is a deceptive word in itself. People can be very deeply wounded by hearsay, as Hero herself finds out later in the play. Arguably the deception of Benedick and Beatrice by their friends is not only deployed to bring them together, but also to "teach them a lesson" or, explicitly, to punish them for their unconventional stances on love and marriage by proving they are just as prone to love as everybody else, given the right circumstances. [*AO1 for advancing the argument with a judiciously selected quote; AO2 for the close analysis of the language*].

- As Hero's ploy gets underway after this extract, and she and Ursula pretend to talk behind Beatrice's back, her words are surprisingly harsh: she asserts that Beatrice 'cannot love, nor take no shape nor project of affection, she is so self-endeared' – a sentiment that surely stings, coming as it does from the mouth of a loving cousin In fact, one might argue that Hero is not just brutal but *brutally honest* with this assessment, which draws attention to yet another facet of deception: that it can ironically offer a venue for an unusual degree of honesty. Yet even if this deception is intended to punish, Hero is ultimately (to borrow Hamlet's dictum) being 'cruel to be kind,' since she does in fact correct Beatrice's self-defeating mindset: 'Contempt, farewell! And maiden pride, adieu!' [*AO1 for advancing the argument with a judiciously selected quote; AO2 for the close analysis of the language*].

- <u>Elsewhere in the play:</u> This presentation of deception as punishment is echoed later in the play by the punishment of Claudio by Leonato for the jilting of his daughter. As penance for his being the cause of Hero's apparent death, Claudio is made to make amends by marrying a stranger, albeit an imaginary relation of Hero's. Shakespeare's presentation of deception as a punishment can be seen in several of his plays, including Oberon's magical punishment of Titania for her obstinacy in *A Midsummer Night's Dream*, and Helena and Diana's deception of Bertram as a penalty for his disloyalty in *All's Well That Ends*

*Well. [AO3 for placing the text in literary-historical context]*.

## Conclusion

---

"There are so many instances of deception in *Much Ado About Nothing* that it is almost dizzying; the audience can exclaim with the heroine in *Romeo And Juliet*: 'O that deceit should dwell in such a glorious palace!' Shakespeare's presentation of deception appears to be many-layered; multiple plot strands concerning deceit and substitutions wind through the drama and cause joy or misery according to their progenitors' plans. All the major characters are in some way involved in deception, whether plotting it, falling victim to it, or helping to resolve the problems it causes – and sometimes all three."

---

A frieze based on *Much Ado About Nothing* in London. It depicts the sequence in which Leonato, Don Pedro & Claudio instigate their scheme designed to manipulate Benedick.

READ THE FOLLOWING EXTRACT FROM
ACT 3 SCENE 3 OF MUCH ADO ABOUT
NOTHING AND THEN ANSWER THE
QUESTION THAT FOLLOWS.

**AT THIS POINT in the play, the Watch and their
Constable are organising their night's duties.**

**DOGBERRY**

You are thought here to be the most senseless and fit
    man for the constable of the watch; therefore bear
    you the lantern. This is your charge: you shall
    comprehend all vagrom men; you are to bid any
    man stand, in the prince's name.

**Second Watchman**

How if a' will not stand?

**DOGBERRY**

Why, then, take no note of him, but let him go; and
    presently call the rest of the watch together and
    thank God you are rid of a knave.

**VERGES**

If he will not stand when he is bidden, he is none of the
    prince's subjects.

**DOGBERRY**

True, and they are to meddle with none but the prince's
subjects. You shall also make no noise in the streets;
for, for the watch to babble and to talk is most
tolerable and not to be endured.

**Watchman**

We will rather sleep than talk: we know what belongs
to a watch.

**DOGBERRY**

Why, you speak like an ancient and most quiet
watchman; for I cannot see how sleeping should
offend: only, have a care that your bills be not
stolen.

---

**Starting with this passage, explore how far
you think Shakespeare portrays Dogberry
as an incompetent officer.**

**Write about:**

**• how far Shakespeare presents Dogberry as
an incompetent officer in this extract**

**• how far Shakespeare presents Dogberry as
an incompetent officer in the play as a
whole**

---

## Introduction

In a bid to score early AO3 marks, and to start the essay in a
way that will grab the examiner's attention, I have invoked a
host of other instances in which the trope of the bumbling official has appeared in fiction. I have then once again pivoted to a

quick discussion of the themes I intend to discuss, thereby priming the examiner to award me AO1 marks.

- The bumbling official has been used for comic effect in drama from the *Miles Gloriosus* of Plautus in 206 BC up to present day characters such as General Melchett in *Blackadder Goes Forth*. Shakespeare knew this was a popular type to amuse audiences, and six years after *Much Ado About Nothing*, he repeated the archetype in the character of Constable Elbow in *Measure For Measure*. Yet although Dogberry has the traditional character traits of gullibility and boastfulness, arguably Shakespeare portrays him as a man we can laugh at while appreciating his saving graces.

**Theme/Paragraph One: The extract emphasises Dogberry's bumbling inefficiency by the use of ironic humour. Dogberry advises his men to do the opposite of what one would expect from a useful watch. The comedy comes from the audience knowing what should be done, while Dogberry advises against doing it.**

- In this excerpt Shakespeare uses dramatic irony to comic effect, by having Dogberry give orders to and accept actions from his watch which are the very opposite of efficient; which will, paradoxically, only encourage crime. The audience can imagine the chaos which will ensue if he 'cannot see how sleeping should offend' or when the watchmen are advised not to detain a man against his will. A further source of

humour comes from Dogberry's belief that his men
are competent, indeed perfectly qualified, for their
work: 'Why, you speak like an ancient and most quiet
watchman,' while his men, incongruously, seem to
think him a good leader. [*AO1 for advancing the
argument with judiciously selected quotes*].

- *Elsewhere in the play*: Although Dogberry's ludicrous
instructions go unchallenged by his own men, his
orders and actions are astonishing to the more
educated characters in the play. Leonato is baffled by
Dogberry's circumlocutions and finds him 'tedious,'
while Conrade is compelled to call him an ass – an
epithet that Dogberry resents, yet repeats ad nauseam
to great comic effect.[1] Dickens echoes Shakespeare's
motif in *Oliver Twist*, when another pompous official,
Mr Bumble the beadle, famously declares 'The law is
a ass.' [*AO1 for advancing the argument with a
judiciously selected quote; AO2 for the close analysis
of the language*]..

**Theme/Paragraph Two: Shakespeare underlines
Dogberry's lack of education and self-awareness –
arguably two vital assets for any effective law
enforcement officer – by giving him humorous
misuses of language. Malapropisms and reversals
of meaning make him appear ridiculous.** [2]

- The fault of pretentiousness is a classic attribute of the
comic constable, and Shakespeare gives Dogberry an
ignorance of the limits of his own vocabulary
combined with an ambition to use long words which

he does not understand. His malapropisms in this passage, such as 'senseless' for sensible and 'comprehend' for apprehend, are chosen to be close to the correct expression, so that we may understand Dogberry's meaning, while laughing at his ignorance. The exchanges here between him and his watchmen have the question and answer form of a 'straight man' setting up the jokes for the comedian, with Dogberry providing the punchlines in the time-honoured fashion of knockabout comedy: 'How if 'a will not stand?' '..let him go...and thank God you are rid of a knave.' Shakespeare in this extract, by drawing attention to Dogberry's deep-seated ignorance and lack of self-awareness, is implicitly exposing Dogberry's ill-suitedness to his professional role. [*AO1 for advancing the argument with a judiciously selected quote; AO2 for the close analysis of the language*].

- *Elsewhere in the play*: It could be argued, however, that occasionally Shakespeare gives Dogberry a speech which is funny in a clever way. When the constable refers to letting a thief 'Show himself what he is, and steal out of your company' the audience might wonder if there is real sharpness behind the boorishness; or is he perhaps only witty by chance? [*AO1 for advancing the argument with a judiciously selected quote; AO2 for the close analysis of the language*].

**Theme/Paragraph Three: Dogberry is certainly absurd, but in this extract and throughout the play he does mean well. Shakespeare does not present**

**him as venal or corrupt or violent, which a constable might have been in his position.**

- As ridiculously as Dogberry is portrayed in the play, Shakespeare does not seem to want his audience to dislike him. There are mitigating characteristics about him which keep the laughter fond rather than malicious. Dogberry does not appear cowardly like some stock comic officials in classic literature, nor is he dishonest or brutal. In the sixteenth century constables were recruited by the parish and were unpaid, unsupervised by the courts until cases came to trial, and allowed to mete out any 'necessary' violence, so the reasons and opportunity to be corrupt or cruel were many. Yet Dogberry is presented as dedicated to his job, despite his stupidity, and wishes his men to be likewise: 'Adieu; be vigilant, I beseech you.' [*AO1 for advancing the argument with a judiciously selected quote; AO3 for placing the text in historical context*].

## Conclusion

I have one final argument up my sleeve – namely that in a very real sense, Dogberry, in spite of his lack of verbal dexterity, *does* succeed in his mission, which thus suggests that he *is* competent at his job.

---

"The duties of a constable in charge of a watch were legion. These men were in charge of public safety, crime prevention and detection, fire watch, criminal apprehension, clearing the streets of drunks and vagrants, preventing and policing riots – and yet Shakespeare initially portrays Dogberry as an incompetent, delusional simpleton. Yet it can be argued that this is only the surface presentation, for Dogberry succeeds in the task of exonerating Hero, and can actually be seen as the nemesis of Don John and his accomplices.[3] Despite his failures of language and good sense, he gets the job done in the end and is finally appreciated by Leonato, who says gratefully 'I thank thee for thy care and honest pains.' In the denouement, Dogberry has emerged as competent after all."

READ THE FOLLOWING EXTRACT FROM
ACT 4 SCENE 1 OF MUCH ADO ABOUT
NOTHING AND ANSWER THE QUESTION
THAT FOLLOWS.

**THIS EXTRACT COMES DIRECTLY after Hero has been jilted by Claudio on the strength of Don John's false accusations.**

### LEONATO

Do not live, Hero; do not ope thine eyes:
For, did I think thou wouldst not quickly die,
Thought I thy spirits were stronger than thy shames,
Myself would, on the rearward of reproaches,
Strike at thy life. Grieved I, I had but one?
Chid I for that at frugal nature's frame?
O, one too much by thee! Why had I one?
Why ever wast thou lovely in my eyes?
Why had I not with charitable hand
Took up a beggar's issue at my gates,
Who smirch'd thus and mired with infamy,
I might have said 'No part of it is mine;
This shame derives itself from unknown loins'?
But mine and mine I loved and mine I praised
And mine that I was proud on, mine so much

That I myself was to myself not mine,
Valuing of her,--why, she, O, she is fallen
Into a pit of ink, that the wide sea
Hath drops too few to wash her clean again
And salt too little which may season give
To her foul-tainted flesh!

---

**Explore how far Shakespeare portrays Leonato as a loving father.**

**Write about:**

**• how far Shakespeare presents Leonato as a loving father in this extract**

**• how far Shakespeare presents Leonato as a loving father in the play as a whole**

---

## Introduction

---

"Fatherly love, and a father's responsibility for his daughters in particular, is a subject Shakespeare returned to frequently in both comic and tragic dramas. Lord Capulet in *Romeo and Juliet*, Egeus in *A Midsummer Night's Dream*, and King Lear in the eponymous play all have difficulties with recalcitrant daughters.[1] Hero, however, is presented as obedient and submissive, so it could be considered that any problems Leonato has as a loving father would be those of his own making.[2] Love takes many forms, and Leonato's love seems to be of the changeable kind, dependent on circumstances, as was perhaps the norm for a parent of his era. His expectations of Hero befit his status as the maker of every decision for his daughter's future."

---

## Theme/Paragraph One: The extent of Leonato's devastation at the apparent loss of his daughter's honour might be taken to imply that he was a very loving father until the slander against her.

- This monologue comes in the structure of the play directly after the climactic scene of Hero's jilting, and the intense emotion of Leonato's speech makes it read almost like a cry of pain. The father even threatens to kill his child himself; he would 'Strike at thy life' if she does not do what he wishes and simply die of shame. That the words 'Strike at' constitute a spondee adds further emphasis, since it ensures the metre mirrors the aggression encoded in this comment.[3] However, the use of iambic pentameter (used several times in the play to express strong dramatic emotion), combined with his exclamations of how prized she had been to him beforehand – 'Why ever wast thou lovely in my eyes?' – could be said to show that his misery is in direct ratio to his previous esteem for her; if he did not care very much before this disaster, he would not care so much now. [*AO1 for advancing the argument with a judiciously selected quote; AO2 for the close analysis of the language and for discussing how structure shapes meaning*].

- Elsewhere in the play: When Leonato does believe in his daughter's innocence again, and takes Antonio to challenge Claudio, he appears in earnest about his true feelings for Hero: 'Bring me a father that so loved his child / whose joy of her is overwhelmed like mine.' [*AO1 for advancing the argument with a judiciously selected quote*].

**Theme/Paragraph Two: In this speech, Leonato is presented as having deep feelings for his daughter, but it can be argued he loves her more as a possession, or as an extension of himself, than for her own individual sake.**

- Under the contemporary patriarchal rules of society, wives' and daughters' rights were strictly limited. Young women could not own property, and when they married any assets they brought to the union from their father's estate immediately belonged by law to their husband. These and other similar laws meant that a father took responsibility for his daughter and made her life choices for her. In effect, she belonged to her father and had no autonomy.[4] In this monologue, Leonato repeats the word 'mine' six times, and although he pleads 'Mine I loved,' the love appears to be because she was his, rather than for herself as a separate person. Paradoxically, he also wishes that Hero was *not* his; he posits an allegory where his child was adopted, so as she would be no blood relation, he would not suffer from her disgrace. [*AO1 for advancing the argument with a judiciously selected quote; AO2 for the close analysis of the language; AO3 for placing the text in historical context*].
- Elsewhere in the play: The entitlement of a father to

'own' a daughter's very future is exemplified earlier in the play, when Leonato believes Don Pedro to be interested in marrying Hero. Uninterested in her own preferences unless they echo his own, he tersely tells her: 'If the Prince do solicit you in that kind, you know your answer.' Certainly, this echoes Capulet's tone in *Romeo and Juliet* when his daughter demurs about her proposed marriage to Paris: 'you be mine, I'll give you to my friend.'[5] [*AO1 for advancing the argument with a judiciously selected quote; AO2 for the close analysis of the language; AO3 for placing the text in literary context*].

**Theme/Paragraph Three: Leonato's immediate belief in the calumny against Hero could be considered to show his paternal love to be superficial and without trust, when compared to Beatrice's love for her cousin, which remains constant.**[6] **However, the effect of shock should arguably be considered.**

- Arguably, when Leonato takes the flimsy evidence of Hero's disgrace at face value, his loyalty towards his daughter seems particularly weak and his understanding of her character flawed, as it seems she has never given any reason for him to believe ill of her before this accusation. When compared with Beatrice's wholehearted support for Hero, Shakespeare seems to portray Leonato as a man whose paternal love can be swiftly switched off, with no chance of her being forgiven. His imagery in the words '...the wide sea hath drops too few to wash her clean again' is reminiscent of Lady Macbeth's 'All the perfumes of Arabia will not sweeten this little hand', drawing a parallel that puts Leonato's opinion of his daughter's supposed transgression on an equal footing with the crimes of a murderer.[7] [*AO1 for advancing the argument with a judiciously selected quote; AO2 for the close analysis of the language; AO3 for placing the text in literary context*].

- However, as structurally in the play this speech of Leonato's comes directly after seeing his daughter jilted, it could be argued that his hyperbole is partly down to the immense shock he has received. Leonato is portrayed in the play as elderly and somewhat infirm; Claudio refers to him and Antonio as 'Two old men without teeth' and Leonato is compelled to defend himself: 'I speak not like a dotard or a fool;' so perhaps there is a weakness of mind due to shock that could partially explain his immediate reaction. [*AO1 for advancing the argument with a judiciously selected quote; AO2 for the close analysis of the language*].

- Elsewhere in the play: It can be seen that Leonato, after his initial lack of faith in Hero, soon comes to his senses. It seems his change of heart comes about not because of any proof, but because his belief in her goodness has returned. With this belief, love returns also, and he says to Antonio: 'My soul doth tell me Hero is belied.' [*AO1 for advancing the argument with a judiciously selected quote*].

## Conclusion

---

'It could be argued that Shakespeare portrays Leonato

as a father typical of his time and his standing in society: a fond parent, but one expecting unquestioning obedience from his child. A loving father, unless and until his daughter is suspected of unacceptable behaviour. Leonato is not presented as a parent who offers unconditional love, but that is perhaps a modern idea. His parental behaviour could be considered unremarkable for his situation, and certainly appears so to most of the characters. Antonio remarks casually 'well, niece, I trust you will be rul'd by your father' and only Beatrice and the Friar attempt to change his assumption of Hero's guilt.

Street art rendering of Shakespeare in London

READ THE FOLLOWING EXTRACT FROM
ACT 4 SCENE 1 OF MUCH ADO ABOUT
NOTHING AND ANSWER THE QUESTION
THAT FOLLOWS.

**AT THIS POINT in the play, Beatrice is taking Benedick to task for not challenging Claudio on his lack of trust in Hero.**

**BENEDICK**
Is Claudio thine enemy?
**BEATRICE**
Is he not approved in the height a villain, that hath
    slandered, scorned, dishonoured my kinswoman? O
    that I were a man! What, bear her in hand until
    they come to take hands; and then, with public
    accusation, uncovered slander, unmitigated
    rancour, --O God, that I were a man! I would eat
    his heart in the market-place.
**BENEDICK**
Hear me, Beatrice,--
**BEATRICE**
Talk with a man out at a window! A proper saying!
**BENEDICK**

Nay, but, Beatrice,--

**BEATRICE**

Sweet Hero! She is wronged, she is slandered, she is
    undone.

**BENEDICK**

Beat--

**BEATRICE**

Princes and counties! Surely, a princely testimony, a
    goodly count, Count Comfect; a sweet gallant,
    surely! O that I were a man for his sake! or that I
    had any friend would be a man for my sake! But
    manhood is melted into courtesies, valour into
    compliment, and men are only turned into tongue,
    and trim ones too: he is now as valiant as Hercules
    that only tells a lie and swears it. I cannot be a man
    with wishing, therefore I will die a woman with
    grieving.

---

**Starting with this extract, discuss how
Shakespeare portrays Beatrice as a strong
female character.**

**Write about:**

**• how Shakespeare presents Beatrice as a
strong female character in this extract**

**• how Shakespeare presents Beatrice as a
strong female character in the play as a
whole**

---

# Introduction

"Queen Elizabeth I, the monarch under whom Shakespeare wrote many of his plays, represented a paradox: whereas society at the time saw masculinity as synonymous with strength and femininity with weakness, Elizabeth was the embodiment of monarchical power.[1] Beatrice likewise represents an anomaly, as Shakespeare ascribes to her a number of traits that were equated with masculinity: courage, outspokenness, humour; indeed, she is unwilling to fade quietly into the acceptable norm of female submissiveness. This passage, coming in the play's structure soon after the dramatic climax of Claudio's repudiation of Hero, presents Beatrice as a force for vengeance."

**Theme/Paragraph One: Beatrice is portrayed during this conversation as a woman who regrets her womanhood, as society makes it impossible for her to exact the revenge she wants for her cousin's disgrace. Paradoxically, she uses demeaning imagery to show what she thinks of the state of actual manhood.**

- Revenge is a recurring motif in Shakespeare's canon, but it is unusual for a female character to directly call for the death of a man as vengeance for his acts. Beatrice here is shown as a woman in the grip of rage, so it is a hot-headed wish for revenge, as the hyperbole of 'I would eat his heart in the marketplace' shows, rather than the cold, calculating vengefulness of Don

John. Her rushed, elided speech, her exclamations and her repetition six times of the accusatory word 'slander' show her anger, and her strength could be said to lie in her willingness to let her wrath be seen openly – she has no care as to how others judge her. As she mocks men for their comparative weakness, there is an element of ironic humour for the audience of the day, as all women's parts were then played by young men. [*AO1 for advancing the argument with a judiciously selected quote; AO2 for the close analysis of the language*].

- Elsewhere in the play: Beatrice's ready wit, publicly displayed throughout the play, often tends to denigrate men and indicate her belief that she is stronger than they are. She uses nicknames to mock them, calling Benedick 'Signor Mountanto' and 'The Prince's jester', and here she derides Claudio as 'Count Confect,' comparing him to a sugarplum – something sweet-seeming but of no solidity or real value; perhaps even nauseating. [*AO1 for advancing the argument with a judiciously selected quote; AO2 for the close analysis of the language*].

**Theme/Paragraph Two: Beatrice's strength of character is further emphasised by her continuous support for her cousin. Shakespeare portrays Beatrice with the power of individual thinking, uninfluenced by the opinion of others.**

- The "evidence" that Don John and Borachio invented to humiliate Hero and alienate Claudio from his bride seems flimsy when it is considered objectively. A veiled woman on Hero's balcony must be Hero? The only person to immediately, and without a moment of doubt thereafter, fully support Hero is her cousin Beatrice. Shakespeare presents her as extremely strong in both love and loyalty. These are not pseudo-masculine strengths but can be seen as utterly natural to Beatrice. Her amazement at others' credulousness: 'Talk with a man out at a window! A proper saying!' is almost modern in its simple form, and relatable in any age or century. Further, her use of trochaic words here – 'proper;' 'saying' – creates a cadence of disdainful disapproval, lending her repudiation of this mindset even greater emphasis.[2] [*AO1 for advancing the argument with a judiciously selected quote; AO2 for the close analysis of the language*].

- It might be debated, if the roles were reversed and it was Beatrice that had been jilted at the altar, that the obedient Hero would follow her father's example and believe the lies told. Beatrice, however, remains firmly and independently loyal. [*AO1 for advancing the argument with a judiciously selected quote; AO2 for the close analysis of the language*].

- Elsewhere in the play: At the moment of Hero's collapse at the wedding, Don Pedro, Don John and her supposed lover, Claudio, immediately leave, seemingly without a thought to whether she is alive or dead. As Beatrice supports her and calls for help, Leonato wishes for his daughter's death to avoid the shame she has brought on him. Beatrice shows strength in the crisis when everyone else except the friar is unhelpful or uninterested.

**Theme/Paragraph Three: Beatrice is portrayed**

**here as a strong persuader. By using Benedick's love for her to convince him to challenge his best friend, she proves she is adept at clever manipulation and emotional blackmail.**

- Not only is Beatrice – save in the matter of Don Pedro's romantic deception – portrayed as an independent thinker throughout the play, but she is also shown in this passage to be powerful at persuading another to do her bidding, despite the formidable problem of convincing a man to challenge, and possibly kill, his best friend. Benedick has only acknowledged his love for Beatrice recently, and has fought alongside his friend through at least one military campaign, but Beatrice's will appears stronger than Benedick's. She uses his wish to prove his manhood to her by repeating 'O that I were a man!' and even threatens 'I will die a woman with grieving' until he feels he must do what she wants, even against his own will. [*AO1 for advancing the argument with a judiciously selected quote*].

- Elsewhere in the play: It could be argued that Beatrice is not always presented as strong; and although we do not actually see her crying, when the couple are alone together earlier in this scene she shows signs of weeping. Benedick says 'Lady Beatrice, have you wept all this while?' and Beatrice admits her sorrow and her tears. However, she may realise that his knowledge of her unhappiness could help her convince her lover to exact revenge, and she could be cleverly using her seeming "weakness" as a strength. This heightened emotional scene comes just before Dogberry's interrogation of Don John's confederates, and the comedy this provides helps to lower the dramatic tension after the power of Beatrice's enraged call for revenge. [*AO1 for advancing the argument with a judiciously selected quote; AO2 for the close analysis of the language*].

## Conclusion

---

"The two main female characters in *Much Ado About Nothing* could be considered as a contrast to each other, with Hero portrayed as the dutiful, passive, "feminine" woman, and Beatrice as the unruly, confident, "masculine" woman who has strengths more associated with male personalities. However, much as Benedick's misogyny is revealed to be bravado that he is amused to assume, Beatrice's desire to be a man and her professed wish to discard her womanhood also can be seen as facades adopted when she wishes to tease or shame people into behaving in the way she wants. Her opposition to men and marriage fades, like Katherine's in *The Taming Of The Shrew*, when she falls in love. Yet her intrinsic strengths remain: loyalty in the face of opposition; her will to attain what she wants and bring others to her way of thinking."

---

An illustration of Beatrice dressing down
Benedick from a 1893 book on *Much Ado
About Nothing*.

# ENDNOTES

## ESSAY PLAN ONE

1. The word dichotomy means something similar to opposition. I am saying that there was a great difference between how people in Shakespeare's time believed one ought to treat romantic love, and how romantic scenarios actually played out in real life.
2. A patriarchy is a society ruled by men. The opposite – that is, a society ruled by women – is called a matriarchy.
3. To speak facetiously is to speak with an air of glib irony and sarcasm.
4. Misogyny is the hatred of women.
5. If people are engaging in jocularity, it means they are joking around.
6. Homophones are words that, when said out loud, sound the same, yet are in fact spelt differently and have different meanings. For instance, thyme (a type of herb) is a homophone of time.
7. To be fallible means to be capable of making mistakes.

   If someone is involved in chicanery, it means they are involved in surreptitiously planning and plotting against others.
8. To equivocate is to speak indirectly and noncommittally.
9. If something is ephemeral it means that it is fleeting and subject to imminent change.

## ESSAY PLAN TWO

1. If someone is saturnine, it means they are gloomy or sombre.
2. Someone's machinations are their plans. The word also implies that the plans in question have some element of cunning!
3. An oxymoron is when you have a phrase that combines two paradoxical concepts. To be 'a flattering honest man' is an oxymoron, because to flatter someone is the opposite of being honest with them. Likewise, 'plain-dealing villain' is an oxymoron, because villains do not deal plainly with people – they dissemble.
4. A moniker is a bit like a nickname.

## ESSAY PLAN THREE

1. An allusion is a reference. To make a biblical allusion, for instance, is to reference the bible.
2. Elision is when you remove a syllable or a sound from a word, and is usually signified by an apostrophe replacing the missing syllable. We use elision all the time in present-day English – for example, 'let's' and 'I'm'.
3. An affectation is sort of like an act that someone puts on.

## ESSAY PLAN FOUR

1. If something is euphonic, it means it is musical and pleasant-sounding.

   The other potentially tricky phrase here is *iambic pentameter*. Most of Shakespeare's plays make extensive use of iambic pentameter. However, you may be asking: what does this phrase actually mean?

   Let me explain.

   An iamb is a metrical foot in which the emphasis is on the second syllable, and tends to sound more like natural speech. A pentameter is when there are five metrical feet in a line.

   It is often easiest to illustrate with an example. If we take the fifth line of Hero's speech here, and use bold font to represent the stressed syllables, plus a vertical bar to indicate the end of each metrical foot, it will look like this: 'Walk **in** | the **orch** | ard **and** | our **whole** | dis**course**.' Since there are five metrical feet here, all iambic, it is rendered in iambic pentameter.

2. An innuendo is when a phrase or word has a second meaning with sexual connotations.
3. We've already discussed the notion that an iambic pentameter is when you have a line made up of five iambic feet. An iambic tetrameter, on the other hand, is when the line contains *four* iambic feet.

   The next question is, of course, what is an unstressed hyperbeat? This is when you have an extra, unstressed syllable going spare at the end of the line.

   If we take the line we were discussing in the essay plan, and mark out the metre, it would look as follows: 'There **shalt** | thou **find** | my **cous** | in **Bear** | trice.' As you can see, there are four consecutive iambs, then one extra, unstressed syllable going spare. This is the unstressed hyperbeat – though it used to be referred to as a "feminine ending."

   As an aside, when you have a stressed extra syllable, it is called a stressed hyperbeat (and, formerly, a "masculine ending").

## ESSAY PLAN FIVE

1. Circumlocution is when you use more words than is necessary to say something while also talking unclearly.

   The phrase ad nauseam is a Latin phrase and means that something has been said over and over again.

2. A malapropism is when someone accidentally uses an incorrect word that sounds like the word that would have been appropriate for the context, and the mistake often leads to a comical result.

3. To exonerate someone is to absolve them of a wrongdoing.

## ESSAY PLAN SIX

1. The main character in the play *King Lear* is King Lear himself. In short, an eponymous main character is one who shares a name with the book/play/fiction in which he or she appears.

2. To be submissive is to acknowledge the power another individual has over you and to behave in a way that respects that power.

3. We have discussed how you get an iambic foot when you have a metrical foot comprising of two syllables, with a stress on the second syllable but not the first. A spondee, on the other hand, is when both syllables are stressed.

4. To be autonomous is to have control over your own life and decisions.

5. To demur is to express discontent over a situation.

6. A calumny basically refers to a character assassination.

7. If you transgress it means you have gone beyond what is acceptable or permissible.

## ESSAY PLAN SEVEN

1. If something is synonymous to something else, it means that those two things are the same or interchangeable.

2. To repudiate something is to reject or rebuff it.

   I have already mentioned that an iamb is when you have an unstressed syllable followed by a stressed syllable. The reverse of this is called a trochee, which is when you have a stressed syllable followed by an unstressed syllable. As a result, the words mentioned here are trochaic because they both contain two syllables, and in both, the stress is on the first syllable: '**pro**per'; '**say**ing'.

Printed in Great Britain
by Amazon

78187689R00048